People of the Bible

The Bible through stories and pictures

Moses of the Bulrushes

Copyright © in this format Belitha Press Ltd., 1984

Text copyright © Catherine Storr 1984

Illustrations copyright © Jim Russell 1984

Art Director: Treld Bicknell

First published in the United States of America 1984
by Raintree Publishers Inc.
310 West Wisconsin Avenue, Milwaukee, Wisconsin 53203
in association with Belitha Press Ltd., London.

Conceived, designed and produced by Belitha Press Ltd.,
2 Beresford Terrace, London N5 2DH

ISBN 0-8172-1990-0 (U.S.A.)

Library of Congress Cataloging in Publication Data

Storr, Catherine.
    Moses of the bulrushes.

    (People of the Bible)
    Summary: Retells the story of Moses' early life.
    1. Moses (Biblical leader)—Juvenile literature.
2. Exodus, The—Juvenile literature. [1. Moses (Biblical
leader) 2. Exodus, The. 3. Bible stories—O.T.]
I. Russell, Jim, 1933-   ill. II. Title.
BS580.M6S76   1983   222′.10924   83-11121

ISBN 0-8172-1990-0

4 5 6 7 8 9 10 11 12 13 14   98 97 96 95 94 93 92 91 90 89 88

Moses of the Bulrushes

Retold by Catherine Storr

Pictures by Jim Russell

Raintree Childrens Books
Milwaukee
Belitha Press Limited • London

Pharaoh, the King of Egypt, was worried. He thought that there were already too many Israelites living in Egypt, and he saw that every year there were more. He was afraid that they might join his enemies to fight against him. So he ordered the Israelite midwives to kill all the boy babies that were born to their women.

The midwives thought the order was cruel and also against the wishes of God. So they saved the babies and made excuses, saying, "The Israelite women have their babies so quickly that we can't get there in time to kill any of them."

One Israelite mother hid her baby boy
for three months after he was born. Then
she knew she couldn't hide him any
longer. So she made a cradle of bulrushes
and mud, and put the baby in it. Then
she floated the cradle among the reeds in
the river. She told her daughter Miriam
to hide near the river and watch to see
what happened.

Presently Pharaoh's daughter, the Princess, came down to the river to wash herself. She found the cradle of bulrushes in the reeds and picked up the baby.

Then the boy's sister came out of hiding. "Do you want a nurse for this baby?" she asked.

When the Princess said she did, Miriam went to get her mother.

The Princess said to the woman, "Take this child and nurse it for me."

The boy was called Moses, which means "one found in the water." He grew up in Egypt, knowing that although the Egyptian princess had found him, he was really an Israelite.

One day, Moses saw an Egyptian hitting an Israelite. Moses looked this way and that way, and when he saw that no one else was there, he killed the Egyptian.

The next day he found two Israelites fighting. When he asked them why, one of them said, "Don't tell us to stop! Yesterday you killed an Egyptian."

Moses knew that if Pharaoh found out about this he would be punished. Moses was frightened, so he left Egypt and went to live in the land of Midian. He pretended to be an Egyptian because he thought he would be safer.

One day Moses was resting near a well. The shepherds of the place were driving away some girls who wanted water for their father's sheep and goats. Moses stood up to the shepherds and helped the girls draw water for their flock.

When the girls came back early from the fields, their father, who was a priest, was surprised. They told him that an Egyptian had helped them water the flock. So Jethro, their father, called Moses into his tent to eat. Later he gave Moses his daughter, Zipporah, to be his wife.

One day, when Moses was out with his flock of sheep and goats, he saw a bush in flames. But although the bush was on fire, it did not burn up. Moses went closer to see what was happening. Then he heard God speak to him out of the burning bush.

God said to Moses, "Take off your shoes, for this is holy ground. I am the God of your fathers, of Abraham, of Isaac, and of Jacob."

Then Moses hid his face, for he was afraid to look at God.

God said, "I know that my people, the children of Israel, suffer great hardships in Egypt. I am going to deliver them, and bring them out of Egypt."

God said, "I will bring them to a good land, a large land, a land flowing with milk and honey."

Moses said, "Why should Pharaoh take any notice of me if I tell him this? And what shall I say to the children of Israel?"

God said, "Tell them that I am the God of their fathers. Say that I AM THAT I AM."

Then Moses said, "Suppose they don't believe me?"
God said, "What is that in your hand?"
Moses said, "It's a rod."
God said, "Throw it on the ground."

Moses did, and the rod was changed into a serpent. Then Moses ran away. God said, "Put out your hand and pick up the serpent by the tail." Then the serpent changed back into a rod.

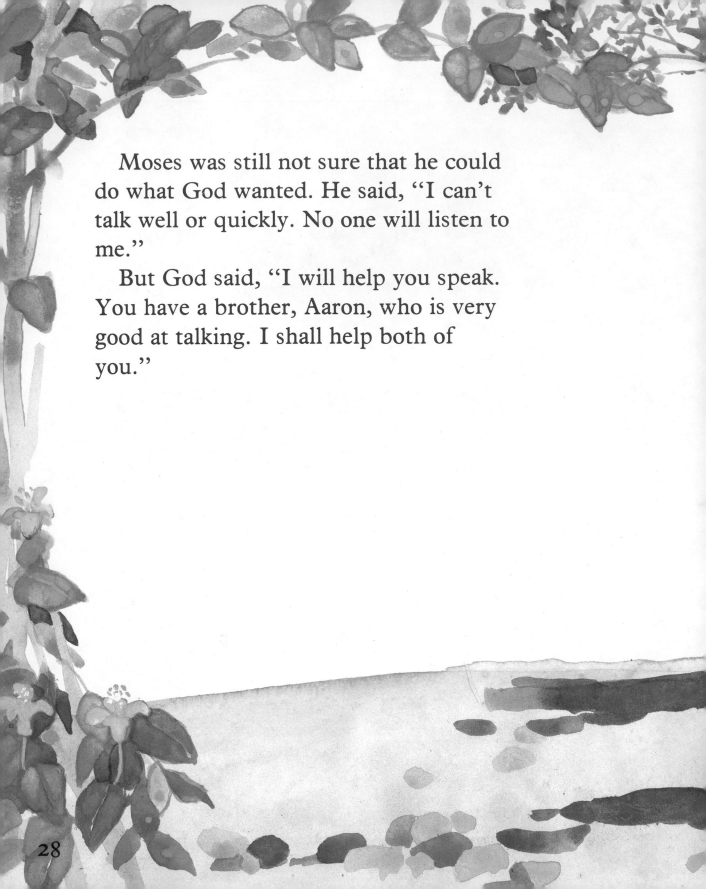

Moses was still not sure that he could do what God wanted. He said, "I can't talk well or quickly. No one will listen to me."

But God said, "I will help you speak. You have a brother, Aaron, who is very good at talking. I shall help both of you."

So Moses and Aaron went down into Egypt.

Moses and Aaron told the children of Israel
that God had sent them to lead the Israelites
out of their captivity in Egypt. "We will
journey to another country," they said. "It is a
land flowing with milk and honey, and it will
be safe and fertile."

But Moses knew it would be a hard task to
persuade Pharaoh to let the people go.

Bible Lands of the Old Testament

Mt. Ararat

Tarshish

R. Tigris

Nineveh

R. Euphrates

Mediterranean Sea

Nazareth

Sea of Galilee

Joppa

Jerusalem

Bethlehem

Hebron

Canaan

Sodom

Babylon ▶

Land of Goshen

Succoth

Ur of the Chaldees ▶

Memphis

SINAI

EGYPT

Thebes